INSIDER SECRETS ABOUT PROPERTY INSURANCE CLAIMS

*What Every Homeowner Must Know About
Their Insurance Policy*

Nikolay Zubyan

Copyright © 2016 Nikolay Zubyan
All rights reserved

ISBN: 1540436527
ISBN 13: 9781540436528

INTRODUCTION

My name is Nikolay Zubyan. I am a licensed public adjuster as well as a licensed contractor with more than eighteen years of experience in the insurance industry. I started as a restoration contractor, dealing with insurance adjusters on a daily basis. The majority of my customers were homeowners like you, and I have witnessed the frustration, stress, and disappointment that were in almost every project I have been involved on. Every homeowner expressed the same disappointment in the insurance companies' handling of the property damage. I was under the impression that insurance adjusters are bound to help clients to restore their homes to pre damage condition and sometimes thought that homeowners were asking too much until that happened to me.

I had a leak in my house from kitchen water pipes, and the damage was extensive. I called my insurance company and filed the claim. The insurance company sent the dry-out company and adjuster. So far so good, I thought, and being involved in the industry as a contractor, I was sure that whole experience would go smoothly. Oh my God, I was wrong. It started when restoration had started. An adjuster from the insurance company started explaining to me some paragraphs in the policy (which I had never read) to explain me why some of the items were not covered, estimates for the repairs were not even close to being right, and so on. On top of it, payments were coming late. That was it for me.

I had heard from other contractors (not from insurance adjusters, of course) that there are public adjusters who represent homeowners to help them with their claims. I got in touch with Steve, a public adjuster, and the result was great.

That happened nineteen years ago. That's when I decided to become a public adjuster. I was sure that by being a public adjuster, I would be able help homeowners like me in their insurance claims, to restore their houses to what they were before. I am happy to state that I consider all of my clients friends, and after even so many years, helping homeowners and their families still brings me joy in the work that I do.

This book is for homeowners that want to get insider information about homeowner insurance policies and the insurance claim process if the property has sustained damage. I think it is important to have this information and to have the ability and knowledge to protect your family and property. You will know who are the main professionals in the insurance industry, whom they represent, and what their roles are in the insurance claim process.

From firsthand experience representing homeowners in their property claims, there is a clear picture that insurance companies are corporations that operate one principle: profit. Waste majority of the claims filed denied or grossly underpaid, and not all homeowners demand their fair settlements due to understanding and complexity of the insurance policy and claim process. I hope the information in this book will provide some better understanding of and preparedness for the insurance claim process.

My qualifications:

- Licensed Public Adjuster Lic. # 2K84771
- Licensed Contractor Lic. # 944187 B, C10, C36, C39
- IICRC Certified Water Damage, Fire and Smoke Damage Cert #180512
- Member of National Association of Public Insurance Adjusters (NAPIA)
- Member of American Association of Public Insurance Adjusters (AAPIA)

1

WHO'S WHO IN THE INSURANCE INDUSTRY

Who are insurance companies? The insurance companies are mostly big corporations and companies for profit. Their main business is to issue the risks involving different kinds of perils for the homeowner's insurance specifically and to insure the properties with a certain amount of limits and cover their property losses. Now insurance companies, as I said, are in business for profit.

How do they make their money? They clearly don't make their money when they pay the claims, obviously. They make their money when they collect the premiums for the policies. This is in their interest. And so the less money they pay through claims, the more money they're going to make in profit. Recent studies have shown that the top ten insurance CEOs have been paid more than $10 million a year.

Now, this is a huge amount to pay for the companies that break even. Insurance companies are necessary to have, and they are required to protect your family. And insurance policies are there to protect your family, your property, and your possessions. But we've got to keep in mind that they are companies for profit. They are not nonprofit. So in their business model, there are calculations to make sure that paying out the claims and collecting the premiums are always for a profit because they've got to answer to their policyholders and to their shareholders.

So insurance companies have to obey the laws of the local government and the federal government. The loans are there to protect the customers and to shield the customers from misrepresentation and being taken advantage of in the case of the property laws or coverage. Now, the insurance industry is pretty much risk management. So everything runs on insurance. Any kind of business, any kind of property is insured. So it is essential to have insurance, but it's necessary to have knowledge about insurance company operations and procedures, in order to be more informed and to avoid abusive situations from insurance company representatives in the claims process. Most of the time they are not fairly sufficient.

And the other thing is that insurance companies are big money, so they always have an incentive. Just recently, a large insurance company was fined a large sum of money because it had been involved in the elections of the judges and the congressmen who are creating and upholding a law to make sure the insurance companies are carrying out their responsibilities. Now, this is kind of a problem now.

The legislature and the judges are there to protect the public from abuse—in our case, from the insurance companies. It's kind of funny that they have the insurance companies helping those same judges or congressmen like that. So, long story short, just keep in mind that insurance companies are mostly corporations there for profit. And the whole model of the way they operate has to be profitable. Otherwise, they won't be in business.

How to buy the insurance. Insurance can be purchased from agents and brokers, insurance agents and brokers. Now, there's a big difference between agents and brokers, which most of the time the public doesn't know. Insurance agents are actually representatives of an insurance company. So they are per se employees of the insurance companies. Now, that means they have to carry the company's logo. They are hired by and work solely for the insurance company. Let's say Farmers or let's say State Farm or Allstate. You can't buy that company's insurance policies from an insurance broker because you have to buy it actually from agents.

Agents, as I said, are different because they work for insurance companies. And brokers are different because, as the word says, they broker the policy. Usually the brokers don't go through the big-name insurance companies. They can sell for different companies, different models of the sales. But the brokers are not employed by the insurance companies. They are brokers, so they are intermediaries between the customer and the insurance company to buy the policy.

Some insurance companies might sell only through brokers. They don't sell to the public directly. So brokers have separate companies that act as intermediaries to get the policy from the insurance company. Now, the main difference to know and recognize is that if the agent is negligent, you can actually sue the insurance company for it. So that means if any case of negligence from the agent occurs, that goes directly to the insurance company or association.

But if your broker did something negligent, you have to sue the brokerage, not the insurance company. It's the actual brokerage. So there's a separation between two companies. If there is a fault for the insurance company, obviously you can sue the insurance company. But let's say the brokerage did sell you a policy that is not appropriate, did some negligent work, didn't do its due diligence or many other situations where it is responsible for its actions, or transmitted fraudulent information—the brokerage can be sued as a separate company. So the main difference is that agents represent the insurance companies, and the insurance company at the bottom line can be held as a responsible party.

But you can actually sue brokerages. You can actually go after brokerages if they're negligent, but as a separate company from insurance company, if that's the case. So that's something you want to know. And brokerages can shop around from different insurance companies. You'll get your policy at the best price, best coverage, whatever the situation is. But agents can only go with one company. So that's the main difference. Brokerages can shop around and get the best options—whatever your criteria are.

Let's say you want to get a higher rating company, prices, and policy deductible. The broker has an ability to go present a case to different insurance companies and get the right policy for you. But an agent can only go to the company he or she is representing—let's say Farmers or Allstate or one of the bigger companies, State Farm. The agent only can sell one company's insurance policies. So that's the main difference between the liability for agents and brokers and the insurance companies that they can sell policies from.

Who are adjusters? And how many types of adjusters?

Okay, let's clarify, who are the adjusters? Now, adjusters present themselves on the other side of the coin of the insurance policies. And based on the insurance policies and insurance companies, the agents and brokers and all that. Now, on the reverse side of that is the claim process, which always starts with adjusters. Now, adjusters are involved only when claims are filed. Now, there are different types of adjusters.

So pay attention. This is important information to know. If you have a property claim, you will know who is representing whom. Number one, insurance staff adjusters. Staff adjusters work for insurance companies directly, so their loyalty and their representations are with the insurance companies. They cannot represent you. They have a job to obey the laws and regulations, but the main thing to remember is that staff adjusters work for insurance companies and represent their interests.

There is a second type called independent adjusters. Independent adjusters are independent adjusting companies that have been hired from an insurance company when it has a claim or doesn't have its own staff adjusters. So it contracts independent adjusters to gather information to adjust the claim.

Now again, independent adjusters can be hired only by insurance companies. So you cannot go out and hire an independent adjuster representative. By law, you cannot do that. By law, an independent adjuster cannot represent you. So again, independent adjusters represent only the insurance companies. And their loyalties lie with the insurance companies because they are their employers, pretty much. They give the adjusters more cases. The more cases the adjusters get, the more money they make.

There's a direct chain from the insurance companies to the independent insurance adjusters. Although it says independent, still their loyalties lie with the insurance companies. And just beware that they cannot represent policyholders or homeowners in their situations.

There is a fourth kind of insurance adjuster. They are called public insurance adjusters.

Now, the emphasis on the name "public." The reason why these public adjuster institutions exist is to give the homeowners and the policyholders a chance to get correct, qualified representation for their claims. This means public insurance adjusters can only represent you, the policy owner, homeowner, or business owner, in the insurance claim. And they work on your behalf. They organize all the claims and get all the documentation. They do everything to get maximum and correct resolution of the claim.

Who are the restoration companies? And what do they do?

You can call them insurance restoration companies because restoration companies usually come to work when there is some kind of insurance claim, most of the time anyway. Well, there is a difference between a general contractor or general service companies and restoration companies. Restoration contractors or companies specialize in insurance claim processing, and they specialize in restoration. They have to take specialty classes in case of fire claiming or any kind of damages that are insurable claims.

It is very important to know that there are different kinds of restoration companies. In the case of a claim, obviously you can hire your own contractor, or you will always be presented with an option for the insurance company's preferred contractor. Now beware—to become a preferred insurance contractor from my experience, you have to present your estimate. Or it has to be your cost of the restoration. It has to be low enough to follow with the model of the insurance company, meaning that they make profit. And in that case, they are going to have more work referred from the insurance companies.

Now on the other side of it, you can actually hire someone from the restoration companies that doesn't do work with the insurance companies. You can hire him or her yourself, so you will be better represented, and he or she will be better qualified to do the jobs on your property when it suffers any kind of damage. But just know that restoration contractors are different from the regular contractors, because any kind of damage to the property, the knowledge and the expertise he or she has got to have to properly fix any kind of damage to get your house in order and have the predamage condition.

Who are the attorneys, and what do they do?

Who are the attorneys? Obviously the attorneys are there to make everybody's life hell. Or if there is an attorney involved in any kind of case, obviously nothing goes right. But attorneys are necessary, in my opinion.

INSIDER SECRETS ABOUT PROPERTY INSURANCE CLAIMS

As contractors, attorneys have to be specialized in property casualty law, property loss law, and property insurance law. As I said, a specialization in insurance law is a little bit different from trial attorneys or any kind of criminal attorneys.

To have your case represented by an attorney, you have to remember that attorney fees are always higher. I always recommend you contact an attorney to get everything right—although if it's not going to cost you that much money, you don't have to. But in my opinion, much of the time, attorneys have to be involved when there is a big dispute between, let's say, a homeowner and an insurance company, or when an insurance company is obviously neglecting the policyholder and not paying a claim or denying a claim. Those are called benefit claims.

Benefit claims always have to be filed in court. And my recommendation is to have attorneys handle the benefit claims, which can be complicated. There are many experts involved, and there are many lawsuits that have to be involved. And for benefit cases, any direction is possible. But again, obviously I am not an attorney to give you any kind of legal advice. Attorneys can represent the insurer or the insured—not on the same cases, obviously. But I have had many situations where I approached an attorney to have him or her represent my client in case of the benefit situation, but there was a bias because he or she was a good attorney and was being retained by the insurance company.

So there is a conflict of interest there. The insurance companies obviously have deep pockets, and they have so many experts available for themselves. And it's kind of hard to deal with them. But good attorneys will always have their own experience, and they work always on contingency so you don't pay anything up front. I have worked with attorneys, and it can be very beneficial to have attorneys representing your case in situations when there is obvious neglect or benefit situations.

A necessary evil—that's what I say. You've got to have an attorney on speed dial, in my opinion. In cases when there is neglect, always have the insurance companies present. If there are no other options that present themselves, a loss needs to be filed. But before that, there are so many options to settle with an insurance company.

Insurance companies are looking for profit. So they really don't want to spend more money on their own attorneys, which will cost them an arm and a leg, instead of just settling the amount in as quick a time as possible. Again, this is a numbers game. Insurance companies are for profit. They don't get emotional with you. Some people say, "Oh, my case has been denied." And that's definitely not the case. Again, this is a numbers game.

What they do are balance sheets. So the less money they pay out, the more money they're going to make.

INSIDER SECRETS ABOUT PROPERTY INSURANCE CLAIMS

Who are the insurance experts, and what do they do?

In cases of property loss or property damage, if there is no agreement between the parties, meaning the insured and the insurer, about the amount of the repairs or what can be recovered, the scope of work, there are experts. Now, experts can be presented by the insured or by the insurer to make sure what is covered and the extent of the damage. Also, they are experts in their fields, such as flooring experts, plumbing experts, appliance experts, or any kind of general contractor who is an expert in his or her field.

In order to be an expert, you have to be really qualified. You've got to have a lot of years of experience. Experts can be presented during the time of the insurance claim, and also they can be presented in the time of the lawsuits or anything else like that that happens. I personally have dealt with a lot of insurance company experts who are really honorable people, and they do their jobs correctly. And I would say that most of the time, they overrule the insurance company's original assessments. Recently, we had a flooring damage that the insurance company didn't want to pay for the full replacement of because there was no way to replace any portion of it, and that's what they were willing to pay.

Now, I requested an expert, and they sent out a very nice gentleman, and he obviously was an expert. And he concurred with me that the whole floor needed to be replaced. There was no way to match it. And what I've noticed is that the experienced ones are always honest. There are some guys out there who will pass on you. But in my career and in the cases that I have dealt with them, I recommend experts because I am an expert in my field also. And I am a general contractor and electrical, plumbing, and roofing contractor with more than twenty-five years of experience. I can kind of speak the same language with the insurance experts and get them to relay my point the way they understand it.

Most of the time, experts aren't necessary. And again, if there is a disagreement, you can hire your own expert, and they can hire their own expert. Now, if they are disagreeing, there is an umpire, which we will speak about in the next chapter about homeowner's insurance. You can definitely get them as an arbiter or a third party to take a look at both of the claims and make a decision. So let's move on to that. Right now, just know that there are experts in their fields, and they specialize in their own niches.

Who are the mortgage companies, and what do they do?

Well, okay, mortgage companies are what they are. They are actually lending money for you to buy a property. But you will ask what role they play in your insurance. This is not information about the mortgage industry. Now keep in mind, there is no law that is requiring you to have insurance on your property. But there are requirements from your mortgage company to carry insurance policies on your property to protect your investments because they're lending money and they take your property as a collateral until you've paid it off.

You have to have insurance, obviously. It's necessary in one of the conditions in their loans, to carry the insurance policy that is going to cover the property. That is collateral for them. So that's one of the main reasons when people buy houses, before they close escrow, they've got to have insurance. Otherwise, the loan will not close. So one of the main reasons mortgage companies involve the insurance industry is because they want to protect their investments on properties that they're lending money on.

Now on the claims side, mortgage companies, there is such a thing called the mortgage clause. Now, the mortgage clause is there to protect the mortgage company. There was a time when there were no mortgage clauses. Without them, when people had big damage on their properties, they got paid by insurance companies. They took the money, and they foreclosed on the property. Now mortgage companies had the foreclosed property with catastrophic damage to the property, which they pretty much lost an arm and a leg on, not just on the side of the foreclosure but on the side of the property being damaged.

So there is a law in the books that's called the mortgage clause. Every time an insurance company issues checks of more than $5,000 or pays out more than $10,000, it has to include the mortgage company. Now, dealing with insurance companies can be a tedious process. We will discuss that process when we get to the chapter where we're going to discuss the claim process and how to deal with the insurance company. Just know that insurance companies are fully involved in the property claim process and by law, they have to be notified with the insured and what's going on with the claim. That will be the conclusion of this chapter, and hopefully you've learned who the insurance companies are, what they do, what their main goal is, who the players are or who's who in the insurance industry, and who are brokers, agents, adjusters, restoration companies, attorneys, experts, and mortgage companies.

Those are the main professionals who are involved with insurance companies and claims. Obviously, there is a back to every front, which means there are underwriters and there are professionals that usually we, as homeowners or property owners, don't get to deal with most of the time. But these are the professionals who are there in the first place, and when you have a claim, most of the time you will deal with these professionals. So let's move on to the next chapter, where we're going to learn about coverage and homeowner's insurance.

2

KNOW YOUR HOMEOWNER'S INSURANCE POLICY

Have you ever asked yourself what types of insurance policies exist? If you are a homeowner, have you ever asked yourself, "How much protection does my family and property have in case of disaster?" Then you might need to read these chapters to get complete information. Now, there are a couple of points that you want to discuss in this chapter that touch on types of insurance policies. It's going to be what's covered and changes that can be made, deductibles, additional expenses, rental houses, and liability coverage.

Let's start with the first. What kind of insurance policies are out there for homeowners? There are four main types of insurance policies: HO1, HO2, HO3, and HO4. Now, HO4 is designed to be coverage for rental properties, and those policies cover only the building. We'll talk about that later. And there's also HO6, which is condominium coverage.

Well, let's talk about HO1. It provides basic named perils coverage for direct damage to the property and personal coverage and medical payment to others. Now, what are basic named perils? Basic named perils are the actual damages caused by any type of disaster has to be named in this policy. Fire, water, or whatever is named in the actual insurance policy—that's what's covered.

HO2 provides coverage for broader named perils, which are a wide range of perils, but they still have to be named.

Now, the most coverage, let's call it full coverage, is HO3, and it will have all the risk coverage for any kind of direct damage to the property, personal coverage, medical payments to others, unscheduled personal property, and on and away from the home—lots of these types of coverage. Now let's concentrate on HO3, which we highly recommend for you to have, and which also is sometimes called special policy. As I said, it's broader and more detailed in coverage.

HO3 provides coverage for all types of disasters, unless there are exclusions in the policy. So be careful when you obtain a policy to make sure you get complete knowledge and go over in detail what's covered and what's excluded. What are the conditions that the policy has that will be enforced? I have seen it so many times. There are exclusions; there are endorsements.

Exclusions are actually as it sounds: excluded types of damages that are not covered in the HO3. Almost all HO3 policies have exclusions from flood and earthquake damages. You can get a separate insurance policy, which can be obtained by adding to the insurance policy, and that's totally separate, although not many companies sell earthquake policies or flood policies. So that's definitely a different subject to talk about.

I want to discuss some of the perils (cause of the damages) that in many cases are covered in all types of the insurance policies.

Water damage can cause extensive damage to your home, business, or complex. Making sure you collect for every item is critical, as you rely on this money to put your home, business, or complex back to pre loss condition.

There are many causes of water damage:

- A pipe burst: usually occurs in the wall or underground
- A pipe leak: usually occurs under a sink
- An AC leak: usually caused by overflowing drip pans or leaky hoses
- A hose leak: usually occurs from a ruptured dishwasher hose, washing machine hose, or refrigerator line
- A sewer line backup: usually results in overflowing water and/or waste into the home or business

- A hot-water heater leak: this is a common occurrence, as old water heaters tend to rust and leak from the bottom of the unit.
- Roof leak: roof leaks are very common in Southern California, but many times the roof itself may not be covered. However, what may be covered is the damage that occurs inside the home or business once the water gets inside.

Fire damage can cause more extensive damage than all the other perils. Besides the damaged area from flames, there is the smoke and odor factor to it, which can affect all of the property and neighbors. The fire damage usually involves the fire department and secondary water damage from fighting the fire. There are some of the damage situations:

- Kitchen fire: food left on the range, oven fire
- Dryer vent fire (caused by dust buildup in the vent)
- Gas leak
- Fireplace mishap
- Faulty appliances

Natural disasters. There are many types of natural disasters. We have spoken about earthquakes and floods, which have to have their own separate insurance. These are the some of the perils; for example, wind damage or wildfire damage to the property are covered.

- Wind damage can cause extensive damage to the roof and exterior of the property.
- Wildfires, besides direct fire damage to the property, can cause secondary damage from smoke and soot that triggers cleaning and damage to pools, AC systems, and interiors of the house.

Now let's talk about endorsements. When you talk about endorsements, you always think that the endorsements can only be adding up to the coverage. As a matter of fact, in recent fires in Southern California, we have seen that there were endorsements that are decreasing the coverage for damage from the wildfires.

This means that they actually decreased the coverage to certain limits of the policy, but they called it an endorsement. So any kind of endorsement pretty much is an addition to the policy. Now when you have a policy addition, it doesn't mean that you have additional coverage—although in most cases, that's the case.

Also your personal property, jewelry, and certain items are not covered. It is going to be hard to cover high-value items because they are called scheduled property, which also requires you to get a separate endorsement, and it's going to add up to your premium. Now the premium, as you know, is money you pay to get the insurance policy. And added endorsements are usually adding up to the policy. But then again, talk to your insurance agent and explain what exactly you need.

We strongly recommend for you to have peace of mind and to have the most coverage's that are available to you. You have to have HO3 coverage, which will cover your building, your personal property, and all perils.

There is such a thing called ACV and RV. ACV stands for actual cash value, and RV is replacement value. Now, actual cash value—we don't want to go into detail on everything—but actual cash value means, in plain language, if you don't get very technical, that it is the amount your item or property is worth right now minus the deductible, meaning they take out depreciation. Depreciation in many cases can be a huge amount of money: 15, 20, 30 percent of the item's worth. Or it can also be the condition of it.

Now, RV is replacement value: whatever your item or a similar item is worth right now. That's what will be in the coverage. Now in most of the cases, personal property is always ACV, and buildings are usually RV. But you can get endorsements to have your personal property covered as RV. Of course, in any case, we recommend you to have the RV on your coverage, which provides the most amount of money for you to replace your damaged property.

I've been asked if we can change the coverage or how to change the coverage. For changing the coverage, let me give you an example. In service to our clients, we also review their insurance policies and make recommendations about what kind of coverage they have. They should be informed. That's very important. Be informed about what's under your insurance policy and what additional coverage you should get to have your family or property better protected.

Some of these changes can be made by phone call, but mostly if you want to add some additional coverage, you have to call your agent. More than likely within a couple of business days, the agent will be able to increase or decrease the limits on your property. Now, it's very important to know that every time you do some kind of addition or any kind of improvement to your property, you have to report to your insurance company in order for it to increase your limits.

Why is it important? Well, there is such a thing as the 80 percent rule. The law requires if you have 80 percent value limits in your policy, the policy will cover 100 percent of everything within the building. Now, if you have less than that, then it becomes an issue that they're not going to cover it. I had a case where a client of mine did some pretty extensive addition and remodeling to the property, and the client increased the property value.

But the client failed to report to the insurance company. And let's just put it this way: the client had a house that was worth about $500,000 and by the 80 percent rule only needed to have $400,000 coverage. After the addition, the house's price jumped to $850,000. Now, for $850,000, you've got to have around $500,000 coverage. And the client had catastrophic damage to the property, which was a total loss.

Unfortunately, what happened was that the insurance company came out and denied it, partially because it said it doesn't comply with the 80 percent rule. And because of this, the insurance company didn't cover it fully. So the client had to replace most of the building out of pocket, which I hate to see. But unfortunately, that's the rule. So it's very important to remember that any kind of improvement or any kind of remodeling to the house that increases the value of the property should be reported to the insurance company to increase the building limit, which is not going to raise the premium that much. But the homeowner will definitely have better coverage and better limits to it. And again, making a change is the important thing. Any kind of improvement or any kind of additions to the property needs to be reported—or adding a pool or any kind of improvement, as I said.

Now, another topic is what's deductible. The deductible is the amount you have to pay first for any kind of damage that happens to your property; after that amount, the insurance company starts covering.

Now, deductibles can be on different coverage. Some deductibles apply to complete insurance policies. I've seen deductibles starting from $500 and up to $8,000. Now, we recommend having nothing more than a $1,000 deductible. Although it affects the premium, when you have a small amount of claims and a $5,000 deductible, after that you just get a very small amount of money for your repairs.

When you need the funds to repair your property, sometimes the deductible will cause havoc. So we definitely recommend having around a $1,000 deductible, which is middle of the road. The other main thing to remember about the insurance coverage is that insurance policies do not cover mechanical damages to the property. They usually cover secondary damages. For example, if your pipe bursts and it causes damage to your property, whatever has been damaged because of the pipe will be covered as long as it's accidental and sudden. That's very important to remember.

Accidental and sudden—that's a condition on the homeowner's insurance policy. You need to know that if you have damage that is happening for a while, for a long time, that might not be the situation that is going to be covered. Let's say you have a small leak, a dripping leak. It keeps dripping for a long time, months or more, and that causes damage to your cabinets or tile. Or let's say you have a dripping pipe inside a wall—it is not burst but has a small drip—that's going to be hard to prove when you have a small amount of damage to the property caused by an ongoing situation. The insurance company will usually deny your claim.

And so you've got to remember that whatever happens to your property has to be sudden and accidental. Sudden and accidental damage can be caused by falling objects—for example, if something fell out of your hand and damaged your cabinet or damaged your tile or anything else. That obviously covers it. Now you may be at fault—I'm not saying that whatever happened was intentional—but if it's accidental, it doesn't matter. Let's say a kid was playing inside a tub and turned on the faucet and the cupboard fell. There it's covered because it's accidental.

Now let's say outside the house you have a barbecue, and you have a fire, and that fire damages siding. That's also covered because that's sudden and accidental, as long as it's unintentional. Otherwise, it's fraud or illegal. Anything sudden or accidental will be covered. So the main thing to remember is that every damage has to be sudden and accidental or an act of God.

There are other types of accidents that are also sudden and accidental, like water. Let's say you have rain or high winds or wildfires. They're also covered, but they're also sudden and accidental. There is nothing preventative that could have been done to prevent that accident.

Additional living coverage is included in your policy. It's a good thing to have, and I've seen it in the policy declaration page. Let's talk about the declaration page for a minute. The declaration page is pretty much the coverage page. It shows all your limits of the policy and also the deductibles. And so it's very important to remember that in the declaration page, you might see A, B, C, D, E, and F sections. Usually this is the sequence. Coverage A is for dwelling, meaning your house pretty much. It's the main building with attached garage or anything attached to it.

So that's a main attachment. Now, coverage B is other structures, usually a detached garage and, let's say, pool house, guest house, shed, that sort of thing. And usually it covers 10 percent of the coverage A. So if you have a $500,000 policy, the limit of that other structure B is 10 percent. But just remember this: it can be negotiated and can be raised up.

Now, coverage C, which is personal property, covers all your personal property located on the property. Now in the case of HO3, that property can be away from the property. Not all of it. There are some limits to it. I think 10 percent of that. But that's also covered. Jewelry and other valuable items can be insured by obtaining special forms or additional endorsements. Now, it's important to know what you have and how much your property is worth.

Now, I've seen personal property being under limits, so let's say you have very expensive furniture, but the coverage limits only cover so much. So it's important to go over your personal property and furniture, and don't forget how much it will cost. Add 20 percent to it. That's what I do usually. And that's how much you should get.

Now coverage D, which is called loss-of-use or additional living expense, is important. Think of it this way. What if something happened to your property, any kind of property damage? Where is your family going to live? Loss-of-use coverage directly impacts your family's roof overhead. Now, thank God, this coverage provides that you can have an emergency shelter; you can go to any kind of hotel and just be there. Or for long-term repairs, which sometimes take a couple of months, you can rent a house fully furnished. You don't have to have your furniture moved into that new house. And they will reimburse you for it completely. Or the insurance company will find a house for you in an area similar to your house. So sometimes you can find the house for yourself and live there if it's convenient and talk to the insurance adjuster to see about a rental. But the insurance companies are usually good about it and cover that. I rarely see a problem with that. Loss-of-use coverage is very important to have. And limits are important too.

If you live in a high-rent area where, let's say, houses cost $10,000, if you have $50,000 coverage, it's only going to cover you for five months. And sometimes repairs on a property take much longer than that. So just pay attention to what is in your area. It's a good thing to have.

Now, the other type of insurance policy is HO4, for rental houses. Meaning if you have a rental property and you rent it out, you will have an HO4 policy that covers only buildings. It doesn't cover any kind of personal property. HO4 has coverage similar to HO3 but without personal coverage, which is C coverage. It doesn't exist in HO4.

When you are renting, it is a good idea to have your tenants obtain renter's insurance, which is not expensive and will give them peace of mind. The lender that I work with, the property managers, I always recommend to make a condition in the rent that the tenants have renter's insurance. That way, they can be covered if anything happens. Any liability will be covered. It's just a good idea to have renter's insurance on top of the HO4, which is renter's insurance.

And also, all the policies in homeowner's insurance have liability coverage. Let's talk about liability coverage, which covers anything you are liable for. If somebody falls in your house, if your dog bites somebody, or if anybody gets injured at your property, you have liability coverage. I've seen liability coverage at $5,000. Nowadays, in my opinion, you have to have at least $300,000 in liability coverage on your property to be covered on top of some kind of umbrella for liability.

And remember, pay attention when you buy an insurance policy. Not every breed of dog is covered, which is important to know. I have seen people who have a breed of dog that insurance companies usually don't cover. They are excluded. So it's always a good idea to go through your insurance policy and read all exclusions and endorsements and be prepared. Now, I understand that insurance policies are written by lawyers or insurance companies and intentionally made so complicated that they have leeway and that they have gray areas that can be interpreted in different ways.

That's why, with our company, we always recommend that you have your insurance policy reviewed by an attorney or by a public adjuster. And just make sure he or she goes over everything and gives you a recommendation. That way, you have a complete picture of your insurance policy. We will move on to the next chapter, which is going to be about filing. So we come to the fun part—how are we going to file the claim?

3

HOW TO FILE AN INSURANCE CLAIM

As we discussed in previous chapters, it is very important to know the coverage's, what type of policy you have, and what your policy is. Now, filing a claim is directly related to what kind of coverage you have. You need to have the policy in hand. Now, as we said before, it's highly recommended that you get a copy of your policy from your agent. Request it from your agent or insurance company just for record keeping and to completely know your coverage's and exclusions. By knowing that, you will be able to decide or at least have educated knowledge whether to file a claim or not.

Not in all cases is it recommended to file a claim. It's kind of a gray area. But in most of the cases, it is recommended to file a claim. You can call your insurance company and file a claim. It all depends what kind of damages you have from what kind of perils and what's the cause of it. So let's start with when you discover you have damage to your property and what to do to file a claim.

The number one procedure you have to do, which is also a requirement in your policy, is to take preventative measures to stop the continuation of damage to the property. That means if you have water damage such as a burst pipe, you have to shut off the water or hire somebody to come out and fix the pipe. Or let's say you have a leaky roof; you have to put a tarp on it. Or if you have wind damage from the roof or you have broken windows and doors, you have to board them up.

Notice the insurance company will reimburse you for it, as long as you keep the records. Make sure you have all the receipts. That is very important. And again, remember number one: you have to prevent damage from occurring again if you notice the damage right away. The first thing you do is make your family as safe as possible. So if you have to move them out of the house, put them in a hotel or any safe place, do that as soon as possible. And if you need help, call 911 or emergency services. The insurance company will cover for that.

Then you can get in touch with the insurance company. Again, number one, make your family safe. Number two, prevent any additional damages from occurring and call 911 if you have to—if you have a fire situation or if you have any kind of water damage and you cannot shut off the water. Any kind of electrical issues or anything that you won't be able to fix and you think is an emergency, call 911. It's better to be safe than sorry. And you won't have any kind of additional damage or any kind of family safety situations. After that, you can call your insurance company, and they will open a claim.

Now remember this: from the moment you call the insurance company, all your conversations are recorded. So when you call the insurance company, the operator will take your information. It's important to have your policy number, or you can give the company your address. The insurance company can take your information and open a claim. Make sure you write down all the information and whom you talk to. That's very important. Document everything. And take the name of who takes your claim. Get the claim number. And if you need an emergency contractor right away to either board up or dry out, you don't have to use the insurance company contractors. You can hire your own to do the emergency services or pack-outs or board-ups.

It's completely up to you if you want to use the preferred contractor from the insurance company. Let's have the situation this way: What if you notice that damage has happened but it is not an emergency? What if you just noticed damage that has just happened but is not a case of emergency? And you don't know whether to file a claim or not file a claim. Remember this—if you're going to file a claim, it is going to be in the system where the insurance company can see how many claims you filed. And that might affect your premium or your policy.

But it's always a good idea to have full coverage. To find out if you particularly have coverage or not—and this is not in case of an emergency, obviously—the best place, in my opinion, to call is a public adjuster. A public adjuster has the appropriate knowledge of insurance policies and damages. The adjuster can assess and make a recommendation to file a claim or not. That's one way.

Also, you can call some kind of contractor, but I always recommend that you call a public adjuster because I think they are the most useful professionals in this type of situation. They have enough experience and knowledge to make a recommendation in that situation. As I stated before, 911 calls are fully paid. If you're not sure in any case, just call 911.

Let's talk about what to do after you notice the damage. As I mentioned before, you have to take preventative measures to prevent additional damage. During the experience with insurance claims, you will come up with a couple of situations that are highly recommended to every homeowner to implement in case of damage.

Number one, take plenty of pictures. Document every aspect of your damage. Whatever is happening, take videos and photos. There is no such thing as too many photos. Nowadays, every cell phone, every piece of equipment can take so many pictures, and they are so cheap. It's very important to have that documentation starting from the time you notice the damages that occurred in your house. Have complete pictures of the damages that happen to your property.

Number two, do not sign any kind of contract when it's an ongoing situation with the damage, except, of course, emergency services. That's a limited service. Don't sign any contracts. Don't hire anybody in a rush. Just resist your urge to have somebody take care of it. That's not always a good decision in the moment because insurance claims are a pretty complicated process.

You want to have somebody that is efficient and has a lot of knowledge and can take care of your problem. So don't hurriedly hire anybody. Just stick with the damages and follow the steps.

Contractors. Again, just like anybody you hire, contractors are very important. A lot of contractors will come up to you and say, "We'll take care of everything; we'll do this and that." Just check their credentials. Make sure they're licensed. I can't tell you how many times I've had cases when I've been called in, and I checked the contractor, and he or she is not even licensed to do that kind of work. My homeowners were shocked. The contractor didn't do a good job, and the contractor is more motivated by profit than by fixing the client's house or taking care of ongoing problems.

Again, don't hurry. Take it one thing at a time. Take a lot of pictures and documentation. Whoever you talk to in any communications with an adjuster, get it in writing. Do not believe or trust anybody for that matter; they can orally promise you something, but that means nothing. They can just refuse an oral promise. So make sure you have all the communications in writing. And get everything in order and have everything on hand.

Also, do not hurriedly hire any public adjusters at the time. Do your due diligence because they will come to you, especially when you need emergency services. I have seen it so many times with people chasing a claim. They go in when the homeowners are most vulnerable, meaning they have some chaotic situation and they don't know what to do or who to call or what's the next step. There are too many people involved in the process.

Just step back, take your time, and make sure all the steps that I just said are followed. And when a public adjuster comes to you, check his or her credentials and make sure he or she is licensed. It's easy to do. Make sure it's him or her in person. All the public adjusters have photo ID from the insurance department and can be easily verified. And make sure they know what they're doing.

In my career, I have seen a public adjuster know nothing about construction or know nothing about restoration. Now, restoration and the adjusting process are interconnected because public adjusters do their own estimates. If they have no knowledge or experience with the construction side of it, they're going to be lacking for the experience that they can assist you more in case of your claim.

The due diligence is recommended. And I'm going to be a little biased at this moment, but I can't tell you how many times it makes a huge, drastic difference when the homeowner first calls a public adjuster. I can understand you can't have the public adjuster on your mind all the time. But just know this—public adjusters are the people that can represent homeowners. They are the only professionals who can do that. Their interests are aligned with the homeowner's interest. And they are the only professionals in this whole process that can help you.

You can call them directly. They can open a claim for you. You can file the claim within six or seven months after damage; obviously, it's not recommended. It is recommended that you call the insurance company right away. But I had damages that happened six months ago, and I had to open a claim—obviously not the results that we were hoping for. But the insurance company had to cover it, and we got a pretty nice settlement that everything had been taken care of.

The other issue with the insurance claim side of it is that the damage might be ongoing. And this is the game with insurance companies. They will come and say, "We are not going to cover that. This is a denied claim." It was an ongoing situation, and it was not sudden or accidental.

Don't believe that. Don't stress about it. This is something that insurance companies do. If the damage was happening and you had no reasonable way to notice that the damage or the leak or whatever was ongoing, the insurance company has to cover it because that is sudden and accidental. So contact the public adjuster when you see any kind of damage to your property. I think that's the best option. Just have him or her take care of it for you.

I had many cases when damage to the property had been caused by a third party, such as a car running into the property and damaging the house or a tree falling from the neighbor's house. There is such a thing called subrogation. Subrogation means your insurance company has a right to go after the responsible party's insurance company or the responsible party themselves. You can open a claim, and it's recommended to do that.

Now, some people say, "Don't open a claim. Just go ahead and do the work to file a claim against a third-party insurance company." In my experience, as far as that goes, I highly recommend you open a claim through your insurance company and have it take care of that subrogation clause. The company will get its money one way or another. And the other thing is that a claim doesn't go against you if it's a subrogated claim caused by somebody else.

INSIDER SECRETS ABOUT PROPERTY INSURANCE CLAIMS

You pay insurance premiums for that situation too. Get your settlements from your insurance company and let it worry about going after whoever caused the damages. As I said, it can be caused many ways. It can be a contractor. It can be physical damages to anything. Maybe a contractor or handyman did something to your property. So instead of you worrying and going through an investigation and that kind of stuff, just have them do the subrogation.

And again, planning of records. Take all the documentation you possibly can. Don't believe anybody who says he or she will come out and do this or that. Just don't believe it. You don't know the extent of your damage, and you don't know if they will do it or not. Recently, I had a case in which one of my clients had a townhouse. On the third floor, due to contractor negligence, there was a water pipe that leaked and damaged the first floor.

And somehow, that contractor had talked to the homeowners and told them that he was going to fix it, and they didn't file a claim. It was a mess. It turned out they didn't have liability insurance, and there was a problem with his insurance. Just file the claim directly through your policy and document everything.

Also, a claim can be filed against you. That's very, very important. That's called a liability claim. That can be if somebody fell on your property, your tree fell, or your dog bit somebody. File a claim right away through your insurance company. You have liability limits in your policy. Get the insurance company to take care of that for you.

And don't worry if it's covered or not. This is not the situation. Every time you think you have a liability claim against you, open a claim and have your insurance company defend you. It is there for you, and you don't want to take the risk of being denied for any reason. So call your insurance company, tell it exactly what happened, and have it take over any kind of claim that's going to go against you.

Otherwise, it is just too much to file. You have to get your attorneys involved. It's just going to cost you too much money and time. File a claim as soon as possible every time you think there is going to be a liability claim against you.

In this chapter, we have learned how to file a claim and who to call. And more importantly, we have learned how to have a step-by-step process in the first part of the claim process, which is filing it, and the procedures and responsibilities as a homeowner that you have.

Again, take a lot of documentation. Have a certified copy of the policy, and make sure you have adequate coverage for your property. We will talk about the claim process in the next chapter, which covers the step-by-step process to get your property back in order.

Lastly, in this chapter I want to include the checklist I believe every homeowner needs to have to be prepared in case of property damage.

INSIDER SECRETS ABOUT PROPERTY INSURANCE CLAIMS

A Guide to What To Do after an Insurance Loss

There are duties that all property insurance policies required to do after suffering an insurance loss. The Department of Insurance (DOI) and insurance policies have recommendations of what to do after property damage that can be found at the DOI website and in your policy documents.

Shield Public Adjusters believe that you need to know additional insights and recommendations that will help you better protect yourself and move your claim in the manner of your choosing.

Recommendations that will help you after a loss:

- Don't give in to the natural inclination to hurry and settle your claim and see quick progress. All claims take time, and in the end it will be well worth the extra time to get the claim settlement you deserve.
- **Remember,** the claim representative and/or independent adjuster represents the insurance companies. The representative/adjuster cannot by law represent the insured (you). The representative/adjuster may tell you that he or she is your representative, but that is not true. The **only** state-licensed adjuster that can legally represent the insured is a **public adjuster.**
- **Do not immediately hire anyone.** Be very careful and take your time before you consider

hiring a so-called "preferred" contractor. For all intents and purposes, the "preferred" contractors work for insurance companies and as result are often more interested in keeping the insurance companies happy than in serving your best interests.
- **Do not** hire any general contractor without seeing a complete estimate and scope of work. This is your property and probably your biggest investment in life. Make sure anything you sign is for temporary repairs or emergency service mitigation-type work. Limited authorization.
- **Make sure** to take plenty of pictures and videos of the damage. There is no such thing as too many pictures. Document everything and keep a log of conversations, names, and persons. Don't let insurance companies be only ones who keep the documentation. Ask in writing for a certified copy of your insurance policy.
- Put any request for information in writing to your public adjuster and/or the insurance company adjuster if you are going to attempt to settle your own loss. It will send a clear message that you are taking the claim seriously, and it will force the insurance company to respond accordingly.
- **Protect your property** from further damage by boarding up broken windows and doors, covering roofs, and est. Insurance companies

will reimburse the cost of the preventative measures, but it is your responsibility to protect your property.

After years of experience and satisfied clients, we think that after insurance loss you should contact a public adjuster as soon as possible. As experts in insurance claim management and with extensive construction background, Shield Public Adjusters will get the stress and guessing out of the picture. Our team of contractors, adjusters, and professionals will get you the best settlement to get your house/business back as it was before damage, or better. We work exclusively for the policyholder, **not** for insurance companies. **Contact us for a free, no-obligation claim review and consultation at 1-800-397-0801.**

4

THE CLAIMS PROCESS

We are going to go into detail on what happens in the claims process to get your property back in order—get it back to its predamaged condition. One thing you have to remember is that insurance companies are responsible for returning your property to the predamaged condition and to make sure everything is restored and looks the same. There are such things as a line of sight and all the procedures that need to be followed, which is normal for any insurance company. We'll go into detail on that and the restoration process.

Let's start with the process. Now, first you had property damage, unfortunately, and you have filed an insurance claim. What will happen next? Well, the insurance company will send an emergency response. It depends on what kind of damage you have. If you have water damage, they will do dry out. They will start doing the cleanup. And if you have fire, you can get the property boarded up. Vandalism, they will make sure the property is not acceptable. Preventing any further damage is your responsibility, but you should cover it up if it's something you cannot do.

In this regard, I want to go over the details of a claim that I was representing for a client. After wind damage to the roof shingles, the insurance company settled the claim to replace the roof. There were no damages to the interior of the house. So the homeowner was acting as owner builder (which is permits) and after removing the shingles, I stressed that he had to cover the roof to prevent additional damages. The weather was good, and there were no signs that there would be any changes. The same night after removing the shingles, the weather changed sharply, and rain started pouring. Wind blew out the covering, and rain caused extensive water damage to the house—much more than the first time. I was able to get the insurance company to cover the complete damage by proving that homeowner had taken all reasonable measures to protect the property.

It is highly recommended to have preventative measures in place and to have a plan in place when or if you have a claim. It depends on the severity of the damage and the condition of your property. It is always recommended to have a plan. Now, what is the plan? Obviously, this is a situation in emergencies. So number one, make your family safe. And have your documentation ready and make sure that you know where your family will stay so you can take care of them.

This point was proven once again when Arthur H., a longtime client of mine, called me one night and informed me that his house was on fire. Prior to that, we had a plan in place in case of property damage and had all the documentation to prove the condition and presence of the contents and condition of the house. At first, the insurance company was not willing to reimburse my client's damages fully, stating that the conditions and quantity of the damaged property were unknown. I contacted the adjuster immediately and presented him with our report and pictures. There were no arguments after that. I got Arthur's claim settled fully and with no delays.

Now, in the next step of the process, you will be contacted by the insurance company, and you will be asked questions. Hopefully the company will come out as soon as possible. It depends on your situation and what kind of claim you have. And the company will assign an adjuster. Now, there are different levels of insurance staff adjusters.

Insurance staff adjusters, as we discussed in the first chapter, work for insurance companies. Usually, the first time they come out, they are the small adjusters. What does that mean? There are three types of adjusters: small, medium, and large loss. Small adjusters are newbies, pretty much. They have very small authorization limits they can cover, which depend on the amount of the damages you have.

And that will determine what kind of adjuster you're going to deal with. It's recommended to ask the adjuster what the limits are. Now, if you feel like yours is a big loss, dealing with the small-loss adjuster is not going to help you. We recommend that you ask the adjuster politely, "What's your authorization limit? How much can you write? What's your authority on this claim?" If the adjuster is large loss or anything like that, it's great. You will deal with one insurance adjuster. The adjusters rarely get reassigned.

And that way, everything will be documented. It's always a hassle when you have one adjuster come out at first and document the loss, and then no work has been done, and everything kicks off to another adjuster. It just creates a little bit of disconnect—although as I said, everything is documented. The insurance company has all the records. Whatever you say, whatever document you present, the company will have a record of it.

Be careful what you say. Make sure you tell the truth. Fully cooperate with the insurance adjusters, which is also required in your insurance policy. And just cooperate. Cooperation is necessary. The other thing you need to remember is to ask the insurance adjusters for information. Get the adjuster's card and name. And make sure you keep a log of when you spoke with the adjuster. One perk of hiring a public adjuster and having him or her speak to you is that the adjuster will have everything. Where you spoke, what time you spoke—everything is in a log so it can be presented if necessary.

We spoke about your responsibilities and what you have to do. You can also hire a contractor to prevent additional damages. Now it's always been controversial that the public adjusters get hired after the damages happen. Again, all my clients know better now. And before they file any kind of claims, if they sustain additional damage, they always call me first. And they know better now after suffering some kind of losses in their properties and not being treated fairly by their insurance companies to call a public adjuster first. It just makes your life easier in a stressful situation. So we recommend you call a public adjuster sooner rather than later and let the adjuster take care of it for you.

You have to remember one thing: insurance companies have their own insurance cops, as we call them—their special investigative units. They work for insurance companies. They are like private investigators. They will tear your life apart if they see something. So you have to be careful with them.

Keep proper documentation and make sure everything is organized. Again, cooperate fully and have the log of every conversation, whom you talk to, what was promised you. And that way, it will be much easier to deal with them, and they won't create any additional problems for you. So there is such a thing as SIU, which is kind of a scary name, special investigative unit.

But again, they can be ruthless. I've seen it so many times where they ask questions that are not even close to being relevant to the claim, but that's the process with them. I can understand that there are a lot of frauds that happen, and better safe than sorry.

The other question I've been asked is, "Should I hire insurance company contractors?"

We will discuss the restoration process in the next chapter, what needs to be done and everything. But let me just put this out there: insurance companies prefer contractors. Contractors guarantee their work or will not get paid. Now in order for you to hire any contractor, and this is coming firsthand from me, which I was a preferred contractor for a while for the insurance companies in another life, in order for you to become a preferred contract, the number one thing they look at is the cost.

So by saying that, the insurance company contractors have to keep their prices really low to be the preferred contractors. So that's what they've got to do. They've got to work for free, or they have to save on materials or labor or cut provide less than 100 percent service to the insured and the property. So look at the preferred contractors carefully. Not that they are dishonest or anything like that, but the number one reason they stay as the preferred contractors is the cost.

So just make your own decision off of that. For the preferred contractors, they've got to lean toward the insurance company. Put it that way. And they have to keep the insurance company happy more than you, because the insurance company provides them work. So keep that in mind.

The other topic we should discuss is, what will happen to your contents?

Now you have coverage C, if you remember from chapter two. If you have HO3, you have content coverage, which is coverage C. If you have damages to your contents, document everything. Take a bunch of pictures. Every scratch, every watermark. All smoke and soot damage or physical damage for the insurance loss.

Or let's say your contents have to be removed from the property. Now, emergency services companies usually do that. They will remove your content and store it for you during the construction and restoration process. So the insurance company will reimburse you for it, as long as everything is documented. And sometimes I've seen it happen where the content gets damaged.

So it's a good idea to know the condition of your contents and the worth of them. Best practice is to always keep a receipt or prices of how much they're worth. Remember, contents usually appraise as an actual cash value, which means they're going to deduct depreciation.

So keep that in mind. But also, if you have a temporary house somewhere, usually the content companies are going to move some of the necessary contents to the place where you live. So you've got to just ask them, and they will take care of it for you. I've seen it happen many times in almost every case that I have with the contents. The restoration companies always are good to move the contents to the place where you live.

Now, the last thing in this chapter: when attorneys are needed in the claim. Now obviously, it's always a good thing to have an attorney on speed dial. And as a public adjuster myself, I always deal with property and casualty loss attorneys.

Put it this way: when you have property damage to your house (or any kind of property for that matter), the insurance company doesn't send attorneys. They send adjusters. And we always recommend you have the PAs represent you. That will cost you much less than insurance attorney fees. But attorneys are necessary to work with because in many cases, unfortunately, insurance companies don't do their job, and it comes to the point that they need to be sued. So they're called bad fate claims.

So instead of having a good fate toward their customers and going above the contract to take care of them, they do the opposite. They don't do their due diligence in a timely manner. I'm not an attorney, so I can't go into detail on the bad fate claims obviously, but I have intimate knowledge of it. And so hire an attorney when you think there is no other way to go and you feel like you've been mistreated.

If you feel like you've been mistreated, you most likely were. I've seen claims that have been denied or that have been underpaid by insurance companies. If you contact public adjusters, they usually take care of that problem for you. But in some cases, I have recommended that they just sue the insurance company. So the fee structure can be discussed with the public adjuster because it works a little bit differently.

And attorneys are happy when they have public adjusters on a case and they take over a bad fate because the files and everything has been organized and logged. Most of their job has been done already and is documented. So again, attorneys are necessary, and I recommend you use them every time you think there is a loss that needs to be filed or any kind of additional law process. We'll move on to chapter five and talk about public adjusters.

5

PUBLIC ADJUSTERS: WHO ARE THEY AND WHAT DO THEY DO?

I have been asked so many times: Who are the public adjusters? Why haven't we heard of them? Are they new? What's going on?

I will try to answer some of the questions about what public adjusters do and how they can help the policyholder. Now, the public adjuster institution is not new. It's more than one hundred years old. The law has been enforced, and the Institution of Public Adjusters has been established. In my opinion, not many people know about public adjusters because they only come and see them if they have any property damage and they're in need of their expertise and services.

Yes, it is essential to understand what they do. Are they licensed? Are they not licensed? Every state has its own statutes. So let's go deep and see what's going on.

Now, are they licensed or not? All public adjusters are licensed from the Department of Insurance. And they have stricter qualifications than independent insurance adjusters. They have to carry a bigger bond, which in California is $20,000.

And they have to take tests and continuing education, and they are regulated by the Department of Insurance. The Department of Insurance always has the right to do an audit on their paperwork. They have to prove their contracts. If anybody comes up and says, "I'm a public adjuster," they're really not. You have to be aware that public adjusters are certified and licensed and also that continuing education is part of the requirement.

The qualifications to become a public adjuster are pretty long. They have to have four years in the insurance industry and then take a test and have continuing education. That's the qualification. Let's see what they do.

Who are they, and what's their mission? Public adjusters represent the policyholder or business owner or the landlord. The key role of the public adjuster is to advocate on behalf of the homeowner or business owner who has sustained property loss by negotiating and appraising the first-party insurance claims. In other words, the insurance adjuster is representing you, the policyholder, not the insurance company.

Public insurance adjusters are necessary, in my opinion, to represent the property claim and ensure an honest and full settlement that insurance companies owe you. Unfortunately, the need for public adjusters is growing due to insurance companies mishandling of and unjust approach to the claims that are filed by homeowners or business owners. We talked about that in previous chapters.

Let's look at when to hire and when to not hire public adjusters. Now as we spoke, any kind of damage seems large enough. If you're not sure, we recommend you have the public adjuster come out and do the inspection and consultation on your policy and the extent of the damage. First of all, most of the public adjusters do the consultations for no charge. They will come out, and they will look at your paperwork. That's what we do anyway. We come out; we take a look at your paperwork, your policy, the extent of your damage, and what has been done so far.

And if it makes sense for public adjusters to get involved, and if that's a big enough claim that you can benefit, like a homeowner would benefit by hiring a public adjuster, we would recommend that. But obviously it's your decision as the homeowner.

Let's look at when to not hire a public adjuster. If you have a very small claim, less than $5,000, or you have a claim that's just about as much as your deductible is, we don't recommend you hire a public adjuster.

That's always the situation. You don't want to hire a public adjuster if you won't be able to get the amount of money in a settlement that will justify his or her fees.

The public adjusters work very hard. The main advantage to having public adjusters on your claim is that the public adjusters first of all do preventative work, meaning they can look at your property insurance and make recommendations as to what will happen if any kind of property damage has been sustained.

They are involved firsthand with the insurance company's claim procedures. They always see the results of those coverages and the gray areas that the insurance companies use to play their games or to create red tape to minimize the amount of settlement that is paid to the homeowner or business owners. Now, a good public adjuster will start documentation and the logging process right away.

In our company, the way it's done, on the first day, everything is logged, and everything is documented. All the pictures are taken of the damage to the property. And also, because of my construction background, I am able to correctly assess the amount of the damage to the property and have the insurance company pay out a correct settlement for the loss.

The question has been asked many times: How are public insurance adjusters paid? And is it worth it to have them on our claims? Now, public adjusters are usually paid on a contingency basis on the settlement of the insurance policies. So that means that the public adjuster's payment is directly connected to your settlement that is going to come from the insurance company.

So the adjusters have to work as hard as possible to get the maximum amount of money from the insurance company so they can have higher reimbursement rates. Again, the percentage can be between 10 and 25 percent of the settlement. But the government surveys of insurance companies show that whenever the public adjusters are involved in a claim, the claim usually becomes a couple times higher than if it were settled without an insurance adjuster.

There are many publications in the press that reflect opinion of the services of the public adjuster.

> Hiring a public claims adjuster can put you on an even playing field with your insurance company. Your insurer may assign three different adjusters to work on your claim: one for "additional living expenses," one for your personal property and one for the building portion of your claim. A public adjuster will be able to explain the process and work on your behalf handling the countless meetings, e-mails, phone calls and paper documents that flow for a large claim. (Insure.com, "Secrets of Public Insurance Adjusters: What They Know About Insurance Companies That You Don't.")

Most homeowners, it turns out, have only a vague idea of what their homeowners insurance actually covers. Once a claim is filed, the insurance company will send over an independent adjuster to evaluate the claim. But these independent adjusters aren't so independent. Their job is to represent the insurance company's interests first, and yours second. After all, the insurance company is paying the independent adjuster...

So when disaster strikes, it may very well be worth hiring a professional public adjuster as your advocate in an insurance claim. These adjusters specialize in combing over your damaged property and your homeowners policy, and they make sure the insurer doesn't snake away from a valid claim. Public adjusters many times are veteran insurance company claims adjusters who know how insurance companies operate and have expertise in negotiating property claims to make sure you get the most out of your policy...

"If you have any sort of significant homeowner property claim, we recommend that you not file a claim without having a public adjuster to represent your interests," says Paul Cohen [founder of New York–based consumer advocacy website Fight Bad-Faith Insurance Companies]. (*The Wall Street Journal Online*, "Why Insurance Mediators Help When Disaster Strikes.")

Public adjusters assume all of the duties necessary to get your claim processed, including making an inventory of the loss and presenting your case to the insurance company. A good public adjuster has experience in the industry and will understand your contract and the company's responsibilities right down to the fine print. In exchange, a public adjuster receives a percentage of your claim.

"For the most part, people like using (a public) adjuster because they like the idea that someone is working on their behalf versus someone working on behalf of the company," says P. J. Crowley, Vice President of the Insurance Information Institute. (Bankrate.com, "Do You Need Your Own Claims Adjuster?")

> Public adjusters are experts, employed by you, who are trained to understand how insurance companies deal with the complex policy requirements. One way to assure that you receive all that is rightfully and legally yours if a disaster occurs, is to hire a public insurance adjuster...
>
> A public adjuster is an individual with expertise in the area of insurance adjusting. Many people see the word "public" and automatically associate public adjusters with the government. The title "public adjuster" is used to distinguish them from the insurance adjusters and because they represent you, the public. (*Disaster Recovery Journal*, "When a Property Loss Occurs, Who Is in Control?")

The public adjusters are part of a national and local organization for local adjusters. The biggest ones are the National Association for Public Adjusters and the American Association of Public Adjusters. And specifically for the states, there are public adjusting organizations, which are a good place to find a qualified public adjuster to represent you and do your due diligence, do all the paperwork, and make sure all the qualifications are in place. And just like hiring any contractor or any other professional, don't rush to hire them. Make an appointment.

I would say do the consultation, which is the interview for the adjuster getting the job or not. Just like any other profession, knowledge and expertise are important. We highly recommend that the adjuster has an intimate level of knowledge with the construction and adjusting processes and a knowledge of the whole insurance industry, which is composed of different parts. That is necessary in order to have a complete picture of the claim process and what to do at a certain point, so the end result will be better for the homeowner.

That's the goal of the public adjuster: to get a maximum settlement for the insured. We highly recommend to consult at least with a public insurance adjuster on your claim—or even before anything happens, to be preventative. Be in touch with an adjuster. Have him or her review your policy, and keep in mind that if anything happens to your property, he or she will be there for you to assist you, to get all the documentation ready to go, and to make your life much easier if any kind of property damage happens so your family can return to your house as soon as possible.

So how can public adjusters help homeowners and business owners?

1. Evaluate the existing insurance policy to determine what coverage is applicable in case of insurance claim.

2. Make recommendations to improve your existing policy to have the best protection for your family and property.
3. In case of property damage, determine the appropriate value for settling all covered damages.
4. Conduct inspection and documentation of the damaged property and negotiate the best possible settlement with the insurance company on behalf of the insured by working with insurance adjusters, contractors, and experts.

Public adjusters can reopen closed or denied claims within twelve months of the claim and argue the coverage and settlement on behalf of the homeowner or business owner.

So let's move on to chapter six.

6

HOW TO CHOOSE A RESTORATION CONTRACTOR

Now, restoration contractors in general are a little different from standard remodeling or new construction contractors. The reason why is because they have intimate knowledge in regard to what type of perils can cause what kind of damage and what's the extent of the damage, as well as what is usually covered under policy and what can be replaced and what can be repaired.

Because they specialize in restoration, the restoration contractors use special estimating tools or any kind of estimating software to estimate the extent of the damage and to present to the insurance companies. That's a standard of the industry. Also, most of the time restoration contractors are IRCRC certified, and they have intimate knowledge about the dry out and cleaning and the process of the claim.

So if you have a loss in regard to fire damage or water damage or any other damage, it is important to have a contractor who is familiar with the insurance claim process. Now as we said before, the insurance company will recommend a preferred contractor to do the job and take care of the problem. But again, don't sign anything right away. Do your due diligence. You are the one who controls what needs to be done to your house. So if you don't like the person or you don't like the contractor that's going to go to your house, you have the right to hire someone who is going to do a good job for you and who you are comfortable with. They are going to enter your house, so having that peace of mind about having the person restore your house is very important.

Usually the insurance company reimburses for the materials that are installed in the house. I have seen that most insurance policies are RCV, which is replacement value. So if your house is twenty or thirty years old and those materials are not available anymore, they're going to put brand-new materials. Obviously, they cannot put used materials. They have to be new materials with a similar quality.

If you have a tile countertop, they're going to put the countertop back. For any kind of vinyl flooring, the insurance company will pay you for vinyl flooring. But this is where a good contractor will make a case in conjunction with the public adjuster to get the right materials that are available. Usually the insurance company covers all the costs to get your house better than it was before.

Now in regard to the upgrade, I've been asked so many times, "Can I get an upgrade to the house?" Yes, you can, but usually the upgrades have to be covered under policy, which they are not. But you can pay out of your pocket to have something better. But what is more likely is that the insurance company will get a good contractor who will upgrade your material to the better-quality ones and will cover that under the insurance settlement.

So be aware of that and talk to your contractor. Make sure you get everything in writing in regard to the materials. Inspect everything before you issue any kind of payment. And just do your due diligence. No money up front—keep that in mind. And make sure you pay in portions, as the law requires. They cannot get any money up front. It cannot be more than $1,000 because of the laws that apply in California. Also, the contractors cannot get half up front and half at the end. Make five or six payments. That way, you have some kind of buffer between the payments.

Also, make sure the contractors did a good job. Periodically inspect their work and have them do as they promised.

Now, a lot of times, when I have claims big or small, homeowners always say, "I don't want to get permits." Building permits are required on anything more than a $500 project.

When you go to file a permit for any kind of project, the building department will ask you what percentage of the property is affected. It's kind of hard to do because you have to figure out what was damaged and how much work will need to be done. And your permit fees will be reimbursed by the insurance company, and also the building inspector will come out and do the inspection to see what is necessary and that everything is done properly and take a little bit of the load off your shoulders.

The other way building permits are necessary is if you have any kind of codes that change, and more likely the codes have changed from when your house was built if it's more than twenty years old. And some of the damaged aspects of your house might need to be brought up to code. You might say, "Oh, that's additional work. The insurance company is going to yell and scream."

But, remember, we talked about how you need to know your policy. Now, your policy has an endorsement that is called low-ordinance coverage, which will cover 10 percent of your coverage A, which is your building coverage. You do the upgrades. Now, let's think about it this way. Let's say you have water damage, and you have to take out the drywall and some of the damaged flooring, but you are required to have smoke detectors added to the house. Or let's say you have roofing that is not the same as the code requires. You cannot go ask the insurance company, "Hey, this is supposed to be covered because it's a code upgrade?"

The insurance company will say no. It is going to argue. But if you have a building permit, then a building inspector will come out and do the inspection for you, and he or she will write down the official paperwork. And the insurance company, 99 percent of the time, will cover the additional cost because that has been required by the building department, which trumps all the policy requirements.

Just remember this: any laws and regulations trump the policy restrictions. So that means the repairs are required to be done a certain way and to upgrade to certain codes that the insurance company has to pay for. And sometimes that happens. A couple years ago, I was recommending a building permit, which is not that expensive. And I had a case where the damage was about $9,500, but the code upgrades came out to be about $32,000. So there are additional funds available for you in your policy.

But you have to do it the right way and talk with your public adjuster to get the right recommendation. And that's why the professional is needed. This is kind of an unknown portion of the insurance policies that are always recommended to have. Now I've been asked so many times, "Hey, the original estimate was X amount of money," and then when the client starts doing the construction, he or she might not have enough money to repair the house.

Well, you can always file a supplemental estimate to the insurance company. There is a procedure for that. You can get in touch with an adjuster and tell him or her, "This is what's going on." That additional supplemental request needs to be related directly to the damage. It has to be because of it.

Now, let's say you have water damage in the kitchen and originally the insurance company paid you for reinstallation of the cabinets. But when the time comes to do the job and the contractor starts pulling out the cabinets, the cabinets get damaged. Now, it's not because it's the contractor's fault, because nobody can guarantee that the installation of cabinets or any kind of countertop will be the same as the way it was before. And it's kind of hard to guarantee that it's going to be as good as the condition before. So they need to pay for the cabinets.

Now, let's say the lower cabinets got damaged and the upper cabinets are still intact. Remember this: the contractors install something of the same condition that looks the same as when it was new. You can't install new cabinets underneath and have the upper cabinets stay the same, because they're going to look drastically different. So most of the time, when we're replacing any kind of cabinet, we're replacing the whole cabinetry. And that's a very large portion of the settlement, and the insurance company of course is going to fight it because it doesn't want to pay for it.

But most of the time, if your public adjuster or contractor presents the claim correctly, the insurance

INSIDER SECRETS ABOUT PROPERTY INSURANCE CLAIMS

company will cover that. And in my experience, it's always a little bit of a disagreement, but at the end you always get the results that the customer gets his or her property replaced, and most of the time with newer materials installed. Now you can call that an upgrade, but technically that's just the upgrade value. But most of the time you can get upgrades on your property. Now saying that, filing a claim will not upgrade your house, obviously.

Now, the thing to remember is that the third party to this construction process between the insurance company and the contractor is the mortgage company. Remember, we mentioned in the first chapter that there is such a thing called a mortgage clause. And the mortgage clause is the law that requires that any settlement checks have the mortgage company's name on them. Now, why is that? To ensure that the damage is repaired, because the mortgage companies have a lien on your company, and they lend the money with the property as collateral.

Sometimes the mortgage companies are harder to work with than the insurance companies. Let's say you have the check, and you call your mortgage company and say, "Hey, we've got this much in damages. We need this check cashed." Ninety-nine percent of the time, depending on how much the check is, the mortgage company will require you to send it the estimate and who's going to do the work and what work needs to be done.

Send an endorsed check to the mortgage company and have it process that and put it in an escrow account. Then it releases the funds partially. Let's think of it this way: it is more work. It's hard to work with them. It takes time. And you have to know how to work with them, how to talk to them. Make sure you feel comfortable.

And most of the time when I talk to my cases, the mortgage company is happy to have a public adjuster on a case because it knows that any requirement it asks for has been understood. So this is how it works: When you send all the required paperwork, you request about 20 percent of the funds to be released so you can start the work. When you start the work, every time you do a portion of the work, you are requesting an inspector from the mortgage company. So the mortgage company will send its own inspector.

Sometimes you pay for it, and sometimes the mortgage company pays for it. It depends on the mortgage company. And what it does, it comes out, inspects the property, sees that a portion of the job has been done. It takes pictures and makes a report and sends it to the mortgage company. The mortgage company gets the inspection and puts out a request for a percentage of the work. And at the end, when everything is done, the mortgage company does the final inspection and releases the final portion of the funds to you.

Now remember, if you delay on the loan in any way, the mortgage company will hold that money. It will not pay you anything. So make sure before you file the claim or send a check that you know that all your mortgage payments are up to date. Otherwise, as soon as the mortgage company sees that money, the first thing that's going to happen is that it's going to go toward your loan to get up to date. That's very important.

Obviously, there is more involved with the procedures with the restoration process. Every case is different. Every claim is different. Every situation is different. That's how I always approach it. That's why we talk to our clients all the time to make sure. Every case that we take on, we get the complete picture of it at a personal level and to the level of the damages, so we can make the whole case sufficient for our policyholder.

That is the end of chapter six. Let's move on to chapter seven.

7

HOW TO KNOW IF YOU GOT A FAIR SETTLEMENT FROM THE INSURANCE COMPANY

If your insurance company takes care of your property damages and you completely trust them to do so, more than likely they underpaid you. But to be sure, it's always a good idea to get a second opinion and to have a public adjuster or contractor take a look at your paperwork. But again, make sure you have a public adjuster or attorney look at your paperwork, what has been done, what has been settled.

If you don't feel like you have been treated fairly and if your gut feeling is not there, I think it's usually the case that something has gone wrong. Recently, I had many cases in regard to wildfire damages to houses from the soot and the smoke. In many claims that I have been involved with, the insurance companies completely underpaid the insured, and the insured has gone out and cleaned it themselves. And then afterward, it's always kind of hard to prove the extent of the damages because the job has been done, and it obviously has been underpaid. Just have the option to have somebody take a look at your claim afterward and make sure you have been settled correctly for the right amount for your damages. Always the documentation is required. I can't emphasize enough the importance of pictures or videos or any kind of documentation. It's paramount.

And you can always get a second opinion on the contracted work. You can hire a second contractor to come out and give an estimate, or second and third. Usually, contractors don't charge money for estimates. And that way, you have a feeling for what's going on. You will have a complete picture of what happened to the property.

Now, let's say your insurance company presents you with an estimate, and to be sure, you get a second opinion and a second or third estimate from different contractors to submit to the insurance company. That way, you have a fair settlement as close as possible. But our recommendation again is to have the public adjuster take care of that.

Sometimes they pay overhead that might cover your public adjuster's fees. And it's just a habit where the insurance companies always underpay. I don't know what's going on with them. And that's why you can see so many lawsuits and so many complaints against insurance companies—they underpay their policyholders. They don't treat them well.

Make sure you have the complete picture and the right professionals to help you with it. The other thing you should remember is this: public adjusters will help you with handling your claim, handling all the information, making sure it's covered, and making sure you have a complete settlement.

Okay, let's move on with what's really the main thing: What if your claim has been denied?

Public adjusters can reopen your claim, or you can open the claim if you feel like you have been unjustly denied and reexamine the cause of it. And try to get the insurance companies covered. But it has to be done within a year to bring the lawsuit against the insurance companies. We recommend that the denied claim should be referred to a professional as soon as possible. Or they can have documentation and everything you've done as close to the data loss as possible.

These are some tips on the denied or underpaid claims.

Denied claims: If you've made a claim on your homeowner's insurance and it's been denied, don't give up. There **are** some things you can do to keep the claim active and try to reverse the decision.

Here are nine useful tips for winning your homeowner's insurance claim:

Tip 1—Don't assume **no** is final.
Did you know that less than 1 percent of claimants query the decision when a claim is denied? Yet over 50 percent of those who do fight back get results.

So, you've got a good chance of winning if you fight back.

Of claims submitted, 10 percent are unjustly denied, so if you are aware your claim is legitimate and you've not indulged in any creative claiming, you have a good chance—even if the insurance company has said no.

It's also a fact that most claimants who query their claims end up with a better settlement…or having a denial reversed!

Tip 2—Get it in writing.
Insist on a review of the case and a written, comprehensive explanation of the reasons for rejecting the claim. It's surprising how many insurers don't give their "no" in writing, and it may be a legal requirement where you live.

Tip 3—Now check your policy.
Once you have it in writing, check the reason for denial against your policy. Look for **anything** that doesn't add up or make sense. Then query this in writing, referring to quotes from the policy where necessary.

Many claims come down to interpretation of the policy, so a good case explaining why you believe your claim is valid may lead to reconsideration.

Tip 4—Never accept claims process errors.
The insurer will have a claims process or filing process. For example, you need to file the claim within a certain window of time. The insurance company may deny your claim (or try to) just because you filled in a form incorrectly or didn't file within the designated time limit.

An insurance company cannot usually refuse to pay a claim that is otherwise valid just because of a claim filing error in most legal jurisdictions, unless it can show that your error either harmed the company or prevented it from investigating adequately.

(By the way, each country and state has its own regulations about claims and responding to them, so do check your own location's rules and regulations before implementing the ideas on this list.)

Tip 5—Try asking your agent for assistance/advice.
This isn't, frankly, very likely to do any good, but you never know until you try. The agent may be able to help or to direct you to the right people to contact for the following tips.

Tip 6—Call the authorities.
In the United States, call the state insurance department or the department of insurance. In the United

Kingdom, call the insurance ombudsman. Wherever you are, check first with the legal authority that governs insurance about what your rights are.

Tip 7—Secure an agent.
Actors and writers use agents to represent them in the marketplace. Insurance companies also use agents so they don't have to deal with you personally.

Consider hiring an agent to represent you in the claim. Good agents will pay for themselves in major claims.

Many people aren't aware that these agents exist. For example, in the United States, they may be called "Professional Loss Consultants" and charge a fee of about 10 to 15 percent of your claim. They know how to deal with insurers and claims and may increase your claim for you if they are brought in early enough (which may cover their fees). If you've already made a claim and lost, they may still be able to help.

But beware of "no-win, no-fee" arrangements, attractive though they may sound. Before signing, check what the fee **will** be if you win—and who will pay. Otherwise, you may find your winning claim is eaten away by the agent's legal costs.

Tip 8—Consider a lawyer.
Now, this tip is a two-edged sword. Insurance companies tend to sit up and take notice when lawyers are brought in. On the other hand, once a lawyer or

attorney is hired, you may find that the insurance company and your own agent (if you have one) will only be able to communicate through the lawyer, which can be costly and time consuming.

Tip 9—Be persistent.
Telephone the company regularly—every two to three weeks. Be polite but be persistent. Keep asking for the person's supervisor or manager if you don't get a suitable response.

Log all phone calls with the date, time, and names of the people you spoke with. Follow each call up with a letter explaining the conversation and the issue you have with it, and ask for a written response within fourteen days. Then call again if/when you don't get a response.

It goes without saying to also keep copies of all letters you send and to send everything by certified mail with return receipt.

We obviously can't guarantee that these tips will get your claim paid out, but they certainly can help.

And remember, less than 1 percent of people query a rejected claim, yet over 50 percent of those who do get somewhere!

We hope these homeowner's insurance tips were useful—we'll see you next week.

But that can get the insurance company to comply. I have had many cases of denied claims where the insurance company has come to us to take a look at the claim. We open the claim and get the result to be fully covered by the insurance company, working with experts, working with the different contractors, and presenting our case. And we remind them that there are laws and regulations that have to be followed by the insurance company, which most of the time it doesn't do.

And the insurance company has the responsibility to get its policyholder fully reimbursed and get it resolved. So we can talk about these underpaid and denied claims again. Be aware. Know your policy. Know what's covered. Protect your family. That's very important. Everything else is just property. In my opinion, the most important thing is having protection for your family, and anything else can be replaced or repaired. But the well being and the health of the people in your life are much more important than any insurance claim or any kind of property damage that can occur.

So this is going to be the end of chapter 7.

CONCLUSION

This book was written to be an informational book, presenting homeowners with information that is important to protect their families and property in case of any property damage.

After reading this book, you should be able to recognize

- types of homeowner insurance policies;
- coverages and exclusions and endorsements;
- who the professionals involved in the claim process are and what they do;
- how to file the insurance claim;
- what to do in case of property loss or emergency;
- how to choose contractors;
- who to hire to represent you in case of an insurance claim; and
- how to get the maximum settlement for the insurance claim.

After years of experience and satisfied clients, we think that after an insurance loss, you should contact a public adjuster as soon as possible. As experts in insurance claim management and with extensive construction background, Shield Public Adjusters will get the stress and guesswork out of the picture. Our team of contractors, adjusters, and professionals will get you the best settlement to get your house or business back to how it was before the damage—or better. We work exclusively for the policyholder and **not** for insurance companies. **Contact us toll-free at 1-800-397-0801 for a free, no-obligation claim review and consultation.**

If you're looking the best way to know your homeowner's insurance policy and get recommendations on how to improve it, I want to personally help you get the results you desire. So I've put together a very special no-cost, no-obligation, very limited-time offer just for you.

Get a $250 Homeowner Policy Review…for Free
I have set aside time to personally review your policy and answer any questions that you may have.

I can help you make that happen. Contact us at http://www.shieldclaims.com or call **toll-free 1-800-397-0801.** Ask to speak to Rima and tell her, "I want to take advantage of Nikolay Zubyan's free homeowner's policy review." She will get you all set up.

Nikolay Zubyan
CEO/Licensed Public Adjuster

PS—I understand if you're a bit skeptical. Many of my happy clients felt the same way before they met with me.

TESTIMONIALS

After a pipe leaked on our property, we filed a claim with our insurance company. The insurance company sent their own adjuster who, after a quick inspection, offered us $14500 for repairs. It seemed not enough for the damage we had.

Our friend recommended that we contact Shield Public Adjusters. Nikolay arrived on the same day and took over the claim. After Shield Public Adjusters settled our case, the final amount we received was $95700. Thanks, Nikolay.
—Herry K.

Our condominium flooded from the neighbor's side. Our insurance company originally denied the claim. After comparing a few public adjusting companies, we decided to go with Nikolay from Shield Public Adjusters because of his knowledge, honesty, and

expertise. Nikolay reopened the claim and got us the reimbursement we needed from the insurance company for our damages, and much more than we hoped for. Thanks, Shield!
—Gorge Pan

We had a construction truck hit our house when we were not home. After contacting the construction company with our claim, we were turned away. We did not know what to do, and then our friend recommended Shield Public Adjusters. Nikolay was on it. We got all of our damages covered with deductible. Thanks for the great work.
—Ruben H.

After an accident in the kitchen (that is, a turkey fire) we contacted Nikolay from Shield Public Adjusters before we called our insurance company because our previous experience with them was not so satisfying. As we expected, the claims process was without stress and worry, and we got a great settlement, so we were able to get our house back to how it was before. Great job, Nikolay!
—Patricia L.

Our house sustained water damage from a refrigerator icemaker leak. We filed the claim with our homeowner insurance. Our claim was denied. The insurance adjuster claimed that the damage had been happening

for a long time. Our friend recommended Shield Public Adjusters to represent us in this claim. Nikolay from Shield was very knowledgeable and professional. He knew his job. After presenting our claim to the insurance company, Nikolay got them to fully cover our damages. The results were better than we hoped. Thanks, Nikolay!
—Arthur K.

We contacted Shield Public Adjusters to review our home insurance policy and give us recommendations. We were surprised to know that our home did not have adequate coverage. After following the recommendations from Shield, we changed the policy type and limits and feel much more protected now. Thanks, Nikolay.

After we had water damage in the kitchen, we filed a claim with our insurance company. The insurance adjuster denied our claim by stating that the damage was ongoing. A friend recommended Nicolay from Shield Public Adjusters to manage our claim. After presenting your claim to Insurance company Nikolay has got them fully cover our damages and our living expenses. Great Job.
—Jasmine P.

www.ingramcontent.com/pod-product-compliance
Lightning Source LLC
Chambersburg PA
CBHW070105210526
45170CB00013B/757